E. G. Molnár — H. Matzenauer:

The Voice of Fear

E. G. Molnár:

The Voice of Fear

ten poems

with drawings by
Hugo Matzenauer

ARS HUNGARICA
VIENNA

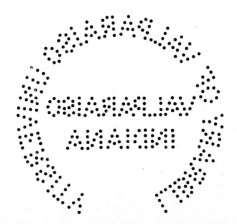

Published for the International World Refugee Year
1959 — 1960 by the Institute for literature and art
ARS HUNGARICA
VIENNA

Blocks prepared by Hanke & Csöngey, Vienna . Printed in Vienna by P. Strohal

OUR VOICE IS A SHY AND FAINT ONE in the great orchestra of western literature. It is neither gentle nor musical for hundreds of years of bitterness have dimmed its tone. Yet it is a real voice, a voice from depths unknown to happier peoples to whom history has been kinder than to us.

But we are eye-witnesses and our duty is to speak out. What we have suffered has to be told for the sake of whole nations still living under those conditions which have given our voice, even those of us who now live in liberty, its sad fall.

We who have kept our belief in human goodness and in democracy in spite of a thousand trials and sorrows — we are confident that Americans who are the bastion of Freedom in our century will understand our purpose. It is a simple humanist purpose.

Freedom and Peace on Earth.

We do not offer solutions for we are not politicians. Our purpose is to present with pen and brush the idea of humanism, of humaneness, and to reject force in all its forms. We have known violence, physical and spirirual, and our purpose here is simply to record it; to bring to the reader's mind the fate of human beings like himself.

Consider their fate and ask yourself — What is the meaning of it?

Vienna, October

The International Refugees' Year 1959-1960

One

Someone At the Door

Clattering
boots on stair
Battering
fists on door
Blows...
burrow in your frame
drill your very heart
frozen fingers
scrabble in the brain
Fear numbing fear
binds closer than bonds
sucks the guts out of you
murders your own man

You know it
you'll talk
you'll say anything
anything they want
anything everything
whatever they want

For the boots
On the steps
Clattering
Battering
Blows...

Two

The Doorbell Rings

My eyes search
frantic for a hiding place
Desperately
scouting out a crack
any crevice
to creep away
There is no cover here
Where is Safety —
blank heaven?
deep in earth?

The ring at the door
has turned me to stone
but that my heart in my mouth
is throttling me
Every nerve
tautens to pain already felt
They are coming to get me

The doorbell rings.

Three

The Clapping Machine

Here I sit
as if I'd grown into my seat
neatly tucked into my straitjacket
And — having to do things having become habit —
my hands — mechanical toys —
clap themselves together
at the word go.
Altogether!
In Time!

The rattle of applause mounts over me
Burying me in nightmare
I can't stand it!
That's enough! Shut Up!
The fear inside me is wilder than the yell
Let's get out of here —
Out? Where?
The need inside me is strangled by the fear
Yet applause infects me too
My own self is conscripted
to pour my spirit down the drain
Amid riotous clapping.

Four

Who is It?

The mind was murdered
a thousand times over
and the brain raped
But the body goes on living
and even feels hunger
But for God's sake
watch yourself!
sitting at table everything tastes the same
Careful, now,
lips are for eating only
Don't say a word
you'll give yourself away
Hush
Listen
In the echoing servile silence
the waiter slips past your chair

. ` .

Who is it?

Five

Welfare

They take good care of you —
— no need to go cold all over —
Unseen their eyes
hold the back of your head
whenever you cross the road
It would be a dreadful pity
if that body of yours
should happen to get under a truck
For you mustn't forget
It belongs to them
Thoughts awake
and dreams asleep
delivered up to be their own
O, they take the greatest care
— you played out old toy —
of this deformed puppet
with the shrivelled brain.

Six

Completed

This case is closed
A sweat-rimmed hat
a worn-out umbrella
are orphaned
The boots tramp away
having finished —
No human creature is here any more
Human?
Class enemy
Reactionary
His two possessions
may well fear
to find themselves alone like this
While one drop, salt, clear,
One single drop
not of blood
Distilled by his whole carcase one tear
gleams crystalline
in shadow

Can the stars see it?

Seven

O Humanity!

Dry and tearless eyes
stare towards the west
staring over the barbed wire
behind which we wait
From westwards flicker signals
beacons of hope
Ah, but how far away that lighted place
How far away the life it signals

Amidst our graveyard hush
the only sound is the crack it makes itself
where a merciless whip
lashes across whole peoples
Yet deep within our breast
wails still the hammering heart
A ghostly army
weeps despairing, a terrible cry for help
sobbing cry
of torment

O humanity! Do you not hear that silent cry?

Eight

Frontier Incident

In the end we revolt
Machine guns
affront your bosom
That cures me of heroism
for life
I must get away — quietly —
Afoot — alone —
except for fear.
I walk
past checkpoints
narrow paths
of mine fields

Inside my darkness
I can feel Freedom
like a distant light.
In vain that brightening
In vain the struggle
In vain the fear.

At the frontiers of my homeland
all hope is gone
at the frontiers of my homeland
Her earth receives me.

Nine

Execution

An Idea has been
executed
Nailed to the Cross once more
and murdered.
Spew of machine guns kill
And trainers crack their whips
Transforming deforming the Idea
Lamentations sear Heaven
hands raise up to Him
the grief of slaves
the anguish of defeat
that spreads infinitely
into a sea of victims
a sea of fear
Only one anxious seed of hope
lives unsullied
One pure belief —
The liberty of thought.

Ten

On the World's Table

Spreadeagled
on the world's table
you lie
Asiatic birds of prey
tear at your vitals
In ringside seats
spectators loll with folded arms
watching the tortured blood
drip down
Even the broken plaint
of groaning breath is drowned
in the discordant prattling
of the commentary.